PAPUNYA SCHOOL BOOK OF COUNTRY AND HISTORY

D0985181

Learning Country

At Papunya School, *ngurra* – country – is at the centre of our learning. It is part of everything we need to know.

We learn about our history and our country from our elders and our community. We learn by going to our country, by living there and being there. We learn through the *Tjukurrpa yara* – the Dreaming stories. We learn through the different songs and dances and paintings, that belong to different *ngurra*.

But as well as learning in this traditional way, we can also find out about our country and our history by putting some of the pieces of the story into a book. That's two way learning: Anangu way, and Western way.

GREAT SANDY DESERT

N

Tanami Road

Lake Mackay

Kiwirrkura

Pikilli

Nyirrpi

PINTUPI

Kintore

Mt Liebig

GIBSON DESERT

Ilypili

Lake Amadeus

Docker River

Uluru

0	50	100	150	200

Kilometres

2

WARLPIRI

Willowra •

Mt Barkly •
Coniston •
• Mt Doreen

Barrow Creek •

• Stirling

ANMATYERRE

Ti Tree Station

Yuendumu
• Mt Allan

Stuart Highway

LURITJA
Napperby

• Karrinyarra

Papunya

Mbunghara

Haasts
Bluff
WESTERN ARRENTE

Hermannsburg

Alice Springs

Areyonga •

Wallace
Rockhole

Santa Teresa

LURITJA
SOUTHERN ARRENTE

Lasseter Highway

LURITJA

PITJANTJATJARA

Our country stretches across the centre of Australia.
We live at Papunya now, but our families come from
different *ngurra* – different traditional country.
At school we speak two languages – Luritja and
English – but at home we usually speak the language
of our family's country.

This book tells the story of what happened in the
early days, when the white people came to the centre of
Australia. It tells what happened then to the A<u>n</u>angu –
Aboriginal people – living in their traditional country.
And it tells why our families ended up living in Papunya.

Area covered by this map.

'A<u>n</u>angu' is the word for all the Indigenous people of
the central desert region of the continent. Within this
group, there are many separate language groups –
such as Pintupi, Warlpiri, Anmatyerre, Pitjantjatjara
and Arrente. Luritja is another language name.

Ngurra is our word for home. It is also our word
for homeland or traditional country.

3

History Begins with the Tjukurrpa

For thousands of years, Indigenous people have lived in balance with the land. They see, hear and know about things. They know and hear with their eyes and ears. They read the country with their feet. They are tuned in to knowledge of the land. Their ancestors are their teachers. The country holds the stories in the rocks, rivers, hills and salt lakes.

The Tjukurrpa is seen in the stars, sun, rainbows, storms and water. For thousands of years we taught our children about this knowledge. It is passed down through families. We learn by doing, copying, mimicking, watching, acting, telling stories, doing ceremonies, listening to stories from country and from inside our hearts.

Papunya Curriculum Project
Charlotte Phillipus

The Tjukurrpa is our law, it explains how the land was made. A Dreamtime character would walk through and make a soak, then move on and make a rockhole. This is how things were created …

It is because of the Dreaming that we are born and exist.

Benny Tjapaltjarri
with Mick Ngamurrayi

We like to live close to our sacred places. We live at these places so we can be close to where our grandparents lived, and care for their Dreaming places.

Smithy Zimran Tjampitjinpa

History Starts to Change

About a hundred and fifty years ago, history suddenly began to change, when our ancestors started to see Tjulkura – white people – coming into our *ngurra*. At first, Anangu thought that the strangers were *mamu* – ghosts or devils.

By 1850, Europeans had come to Australia from across the sea and were living down south on stations or in cities. There was also a little port up north. The Government wanted to find a route across the continent from south to north. Of course, Anangu had been travelling through the desert since the *Tjurkurrpa*, but the Government did not ask them the way. Instead, they held a competition. The first explorer to travel from Adelaide to Darwin would win a lot of money.

I thought the first whites I saw were mamu - devil monsters! They had different skin to us. I thought, 'Eh, these blokes are devils from the grave!' We couldn't believe our eyes, because we have dark skin. It was unbelievable.

Ronnie Tjampitjinpa

In 1860, an explorer called Stuart set out to try to win the prize. He reached the centre of Australia and planted the British flag. But up near Tennant Creek, the traditional owners of the country attacked Stuart's camp with fire and spears. The explorer went back to Adelaide.

Though Aboriginal people won this first encounter, Stuart returned two years later. This time he marked a track all the way from Adelaide to Darwin.

In the 1870s, Anangu started to see more Tjulkura riding into the desert on strange animals. When the newcomers camped at a spring, they could use up all the water in a day. The Anangu needed that water to survive until the next rain. And so they sometimes attacked the camps, to send the explorers away.

As the years went by, more explorers kept coming. They did not learn the language of the country, or the Anangu names for places. They made up new names. They made maps too, so that the cattle owners could follow in their footsteps, and take up leases for stations.

1860s: Anangu began to see white strangers in the desert.
1860: Stuart reached Central Australia. Forced to go back.
1862: Stuart returned. Made a track from Adelaide to Darwin.
1872: Giles travelled 500 km west from Finke River.
1873: Warburton crossed the desert to the west coast.
1873: Gosse set out from Alice Springs.
1873: Giles set out west again. His camp was attacked twice.
1874: Forrest made his way from Perth to the Centre.
1875: Giles went from the Centre to Perth, and back.

Land Taken for Cattle

When the Tjulkura came to Australia, they did not recognise that, between them, different groups of Aboriginal people owned all the continent. Because there were no pieces of paper saying which people belonged to which country, white people decided that the land was *terra nullius*. Those words mean 'empty land' or 'no one's land'. The Tjulkura did not understand that Aboriginal people had been recording their ownership of their country in songs, stories, dances and paintings since the time when law began.

The homestead at Glen Helen Station.

As soon as explorers made the first maps, the Government began giving out pastoral leases over huge areas of Anangu land. The white men wanted to run big mobs of cattle.

The station owners built fences, stockyards and homesteads. They went all over the land, without asking for permission. They did not respect the sacred places.

Balance of Nature Broken

The cattle drank the waterholes dry, and ate the grass that the kangaroos and other bush animals used to eat. Their hard hooves hurt the soft land, and trampled down many of the bush tucker plants. The balance of nature was broken.

Within a few years of the cattle coming, the Anangu found it harder and harder to live in their country, because the bush tucker animals and plants began to disappear, and many of the soaks were destroyed. Besides, many station owners did not allow the Anangu to hunt on their traditional land.

At first the Anangu tried to make the Tjulkura go away by killing their stock. In revenge, the station owners and police attacked the camps where the Anangu lived. They wanted to force the Anangu off the cattle stations.

1870s: Anangu began to see cattle and sheep and fences.
1872: First land leases, Alice Springs region.
1873: First station homestead built in the Centre.
1873: Cattle brought to Glen Helen.
1875: Homestead built at Glen Helen Station.
1883: Tempe Downs Station established.
1880s: Anangu began to find it harder to get bush tucker.

Anangu Resistance

While the pastoralists were taking the land, other white men arrived to build the Overland Telegraph Line up Stuart's track, from Adelaide to Darwin. This allowed people to send messages across the country by Morse code.

Every few hundred kilometres there had to be a station with machinery, to push the messages along the wire. One station was built on Arrente land, at a spring of good water named 'Theyeyurre'. This country is Caterpillar Dreaming.

The whitefellers called the waterhole 'Alice Springs', and they named the nearby river 'the Todd'. The Alice Springs Telegraph Station was the first permanent white settlement in the centre of Australia. As well as the telegraph office and homestead, there was a cattle station, with fences and stockyards. The Alice Springs Telegraph Station became a sort of base camp for explorers, pastoralists, and other whitefellers passing through the area. Mail was held there for people to collect.

Anangu found the telegraph insulators useful for spear heads and scraping tools, but the Telegraph Line brought more and more Tjulkura into their *ngurra*. This meant less water and less food for Anangu.

In 1874, there was an attack on the Telegraph Station at Barrow Creek. One white man died, and so did an Aboriginal man. The Government sent out soldiers on horses, who killed about fifty Anangu in revenge.

1866: Overland Telegraph Line begun.

1870s: More and more strangers come to the Centre.

1871: Telegraph Station built at Alice Springs.

1872: Overland Telegraph Line from Adelaide to Darwin completed.

1874: Attack on Barrow Creek – 250 km north of Alice Springs.

1878: Post Office opened at Alice Springs Telegraph Station.

Missionaries Arrive

Another sort of Tjulkura came from Germany. These ones were Lutheran missionaries, and they wanted to teach the Christian religion to the Anangu.

The Government gave the Mission a large piece of Arrente land in the Finke River area. In 1877, two pastors settled at a spring which was named 'Ntaria'. They called this place 'Hermannsburg'. By the next year they had five buildings, as well as yards for their three thousand sheep.

Teaching children Bible stories.

The first time my grandfather saw the missionaries ... he was hunting kangaroo, and he saw this dust coming. And he run to high hill, look down, something coming here, hide in the bush. He don't know what's coming. Then run back to the camp and tell everybody, they went to the sandhill and stopped there, crying and frightened. Sheep and white people coming but they don't know what that is ...

They thought they was debbils, they don't know whites. They reckon this white is a ghost one, come from the dead.

Joylene Abbott

12

At first the local Western Arrente people did not know what to think about these new white men. But as they continued to be pushed out of their country by the cattle stations, they gradually came to camp around the Mission. The children started to learn reading, writing, geography, singing and Bible stories.

As well as spreading the Gospel, the missionaries tried to stop the police and the station owners from killing Anangu. Over a period of time, Anangu started to see the Mission as a place of refuge.

This stone building was the first church and school at Hermannsburg. At Christmas, the Pastor gave everyone presents from the Christmas tree.

By the late 1890s, Hermannsburg Mission had grown to include l. to r.: Eating house; Smithy; School; Church; Store; Pastor's house.

1877: Pastor Kempe and Pastor Schwarz arrived with 3000 sheep.
1878: Pastor Schulze arrived. Also wives and helpers.
1880: Stone church and school built.
1880s: Arrente began to hear stories about Moses and Tjitju.
1887: Seven Arrente teenagers asked to be baptised.
1890s: More bush tucker disappeared, as grazing land increased.
1894: Pastor Strehlow took charge of the Mission.
1897: New church built.
1903: Forty-five children at Hermannsburg school.
1922: Pastor Strehlow left.
1926: Pastor Albrecht arrived and took charge of the Mission.

In 1894, Pastor Strehlow came to Hermannsburg. Over the next twenty-five years, the Mission got a new church, a school, sleeping dormitories for children and a big eating house. Children had lessons in the morning and did gardening in the afternoons. Two hundred people were baptised. The new religion did not replace traditional life, but could be fitted in with it.

13

A Town Called Stuart

By the 1880s, groups of white men were camped on the banks of the Todd River, a few kilometres south of the Alice Springs Telegraph Station. They were waiting to go mining for gold or garnets. The Government decided to establish a town, to replace the camps. This town was named 'Stuart', after the first white explorer. As the first stores and hotels were built, more Tjulkura came passing through, or settled down to live.

The white people didn't eat bush tucker, so they had to bring a lot of their food from down south. In the early days, camels were used to carry supplies. They came from desert country in Asia, and were able to walk a long way between waterholes. Men came from Afghanistan to look after the camel trains. The Afghans lived in 'ghan towns', on the edge of white settlements. Their religion was Islam. They worshipped together in mosques which they built out of tin.

Around the turn of the century, the dirt track from Adelaide was improved, and transport on wheels gradually started to replace camels and horses.

Town of Stuart, 1896.

1880s: Arrente were being pushed out of area around Todd River.
1888: Town of Stuart – 3 km from Alice Springs Telegraph Station.
1897: First man travelled by bicycle from Adelaide to Darwin.
1901: Federation: States linked up under Federal Government.
1901: About 10 white people lived permanently in Stuart.
1900s: Government continued to give out land as pastoral leases.
1908: First men travelled by car from Adelaide to Darwin.
1911: Northern Territory to be administered by Federal Government.
1914: World War I started: Australia at war with Germany.
1914: School started in Stuart. Bungalow established.
1918: World War I ended.

Going to School in Stuart

In 1914, a school opened in a timber and iron building next to the Stuart Police Station. White children had lessons in the mornings, and Aboriginal children had lessons in the afternoons.

Nearby was a tin shed called the Bungalow. This was a dormitory where some Aboriginal children slept at night. In 1916, there were eight boys and twenty-two girls living there, aged from three to fifteen years. There was not much food, so the children often went out to get bush tucker.

Children play outside the school.

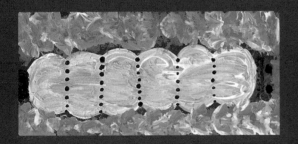

We used to sleep inside in the wet weather. The boys had one room and the girls had one room. In the summer time we just used to camp out on the flat – like a mob of sardines – in one bed. And the kids grew up, you know, like brothers and sisters.

Milton Liddle

Children at the Bungalow, 1918.

Transport and Health

After the First World War ended, things seemed to move more quickly in the little town on the Todd. In 1921, townsfolk were excited to see the first aeroplane land. By the end of the decade, a train ran between Adelaide and Stuart. It was called 'the Ghan' because it replaced the trains of the Afghan camel drivers. A few years later, the first road trains began to travel up the track to Darwin.

In the same decade, health services improved. In 1926, Dr John Flynn set up a hospital in the town. Two years later, Flynn established the Flying Doctor Service. The cattle stations didn't have telephones or electricity, so an engineer called Alf Traeger invented a radio transmitter that ran on pedal power. This allowed people to send messages over long distances when they needed the doctor to come and help them.

1921: First aeroplane arrived in Stuart.
1925: About 40 white people lived permanently in Stuart.
1926: First hospital established in Stuart.
1928: Flying Doctor Service established, with pedal radio network.
1929: Train service from Adelaide to the Centre – 'the Ghan'.
1932: Post Office moved from Telegraph Station to township.
1933: Name of township changed from 'Stuart' to 'Alice Springs'.

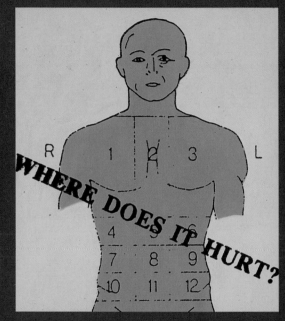

Alf Traeger with the first pedal radio.

WHERE DOES IT HURT?

R   1   2   3   L

4   8   9

7

10   11   12

Alice Springs in the 1930s.

A Town Called Alice

In 1932, another change took place, when the Post Office moved from the Alice Springs Telegraph Station to the settlement at Stuart. People down south kept sending letters addressed to 'Alice Springs'. So the town changed its name. The locals usually just called it 'Alice'.

The old Telegraph Station was now turned into a school and dormitory for Aboriginal children, who were sometimes brought from communities hundreds of kilometres away. Many of them were Stolen Children.

All these changes made life easier for the Tjulkura. But the health of the Arrente people of the Todd River area became worse, as they caught new diseases, brought by the white people, and as their diet of bush tucker was replaced by flour and sugar.

Meanwhile, they continued to lose their land. Houses and shops were built in sacred places, and the road and railway line were blasted through 'the Gap' in the Caterpillar hills.

A favourite game at the Telegraph Station was tyre races.

Long Hard Years of Drought

While life improved for the Tjulkura in the town, it became harder and harder for the A<u>n</u>angu to survive in the desert. In the 1920s there was a terrible drought right through the Centre. The A<u>n</u>angu were not able to live through a long dry season as they had in the past, before the cattle drank the water and destroyed the bush tucker.

As the drought wore on, many A<u>n</u>angu started going to the Hermannsburg Mission for food. At first these were Arrente people from nearby. Soon there were Pintupi from the far west as well. By this time Pastor Albrecht was in charge of the Mission.

With no bush t<u>n</u>cker to eat, the A<u>n</u>angu some-times speared cattle. The pastoralists asked the police for protection. In 1928, a white man was killed at Coniston because he took the wife of an Aboriginal man. In revenge, the police rode out for over a month, hunting Warlpiri. They killed about a hundred men, women and children. After this, many Warlpiri came down to Hermannsburg for refuge.

By 1929, there was very little food left at the Mission. Without fresh vegetables, the A<u>n</u>angu began to get scurvy. People started to get very sick, and many adults and children passed away.

Big mob come in during the drought. All the nekkids, no trousers, dress, no anything. They were little bit frightened, some have not seen white people before, reckon somebody might kill him. People here used to go down and talk to them, friendly. When they were quiet, they would come to eating house, for devotion, nekkid. Native people and Pastor Albrecht gave them clothes. They were frightened, given clothes. People showed them how to put them on.

Edwin Pareroultja

1926: Bad drought. Pastor Albrecht arrived at Hermannsburg.
1928: Coniston Massacre: about 100 A<u>n</u>angu killed by police.
1934: Albert Namatjira began painting.
1935: Mission built a pipeline to bring water for vegetable gardens.

Towards the end of 1929 some scientists in Adelaide sent 130 cases of oranges to the Mission. People started to get better. As the new year began, good rain fell, and the country provided bush tucker to make everyone healthy again. The Pintupi and Warlpiri set off back to their homelands.

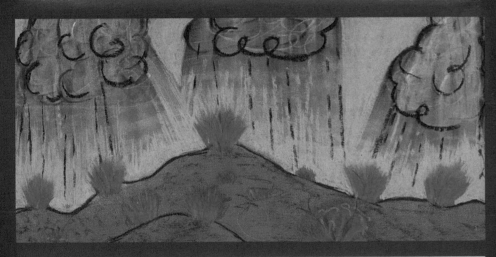

A New Way to Paint Country

In 1932, a white artist named Rex Batterbee visited the Mission, and painted the landscape with watercolours. When an Arrente man named Albert Namatjira saw the pictures, he said, 'I think I can do that too.' Within a few years Namatjira was exhibiting his pictures in galleries down south. Other Hermannsburg artists started painting in a similar style. It was different from working in the traditional way, but it was still portraying the artists' connection with their country and their Dreaming.

Devils in the Sky

When the first white explorers came, they travelled by camel or horse. As time went on, there was a new sort of explorer, who travelled through the sky.

In 1930, the Tjulkura journeyed west of Alice Springs to Ilypili. This was a place in Pintupi country, with waterholes and rock shelters. The white men made a landing strip so planes could refuel there. Then they flew around, taking photographs of the country for a new type of map. Many people remember seeing these first aeroplanes.

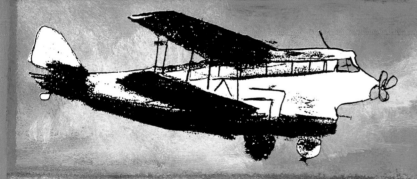

When the plane came, everyone ran and hid behind rocks and trees because they thought it was a mamu.

When the plane came it left flour and clothes. All the kids were lined up to be given flour. Everyone thought it was awful, poison one. Some people buried the tinned food in a hole.

Rita Napaltjarri

I was going along … And then I heard it. 'Oh no, that devil, that big wind is coming.' I didn't know what it was – it had to be a devil! I was lying down in the trees, I was inside those trees hiding as best I could.

That aeroplane went towards Ilypiḻi. It was frightening people wherever it went, all through the west. All those ngankari used to try to bring it down. And then everyone would hide, frightened again. Aboriginal people everywhere thought it was a devil. They would hide in the trees while the ngankari tried to knock it down. They were scared. Throughout the west, south and north it was frightening us.

We thought it was a devil. But it wasn't. That aeroplane was just going around taking photos of us. Whitefellers were sitting inside, looking for Aboriginal people and taking photos. But we thought that aeroplane was a devil.

Johnny Warrangula

1929: The Great Depression began: a time of unemployment.
1930: Mackay Aerial Mapping Expedition built Ilypiḻi landing strip.
1930: Lasseter's expedition set out to look for gold in the desert. His plane also used the Ilypiḻi landing strip.
1931: Lasseter died near Hull Creek.

Spreading the Gospel

A few months after the drought ended, Pastor Albrecht and two Arrente missionaries set off on a camel trek. Now that they had met some of the Anangu from the north and the west, they wanted to go out and meet their neighbours in their home country. This trip would set up a pattern of events which would eventually lead to the establishment of the settlement at Papunya. But at the time, the missionaries' only aim was to spread the Gospel.

After passing Haasts Bluff the men travelled to Central Mount Wedge, then north-west to the beautiful waterhole at Pikilli, where they were made welcome by Warlpiri people.

The three missionaries journeyed on to the next big waterhole, at Ilypili, where they met a number of Pintupi, including Kamutu and his family. The Pastor observed how healthy and contented these people were, and how well they lived in their country.

The missionaries promised to visit again, then set off east on their camels, heading for home by way of the spring at Putarti. On the last leg of the journey they visited Anangu living on cattle stations.

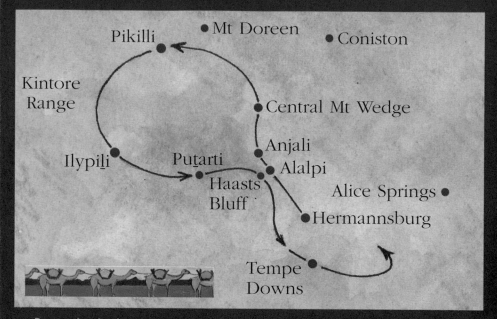

Route taken by the missionaries in 1930.
The journey took 5 weeks and covered 800 km.

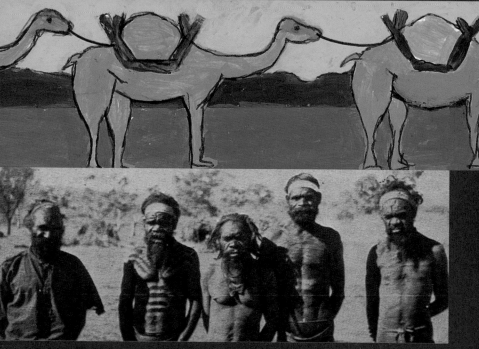

Men at Ilypili. Kamutu is second from left.

After this trip, Pastor Albrecht decided it would be good to send a couple of Arrente missionaries out to live with people in the bush, to pass on the Christian message. A camp was set up at Puṯarti, and rations were sent out regularly for the evangelists. It was a hard job for these men, who were out of their own country and spoke a different language, but they built up a good relationship with the local people. Once a year the Pastor and other men from Hermannsburg visited the camp and other places in the west. Later the mission camp moved from Puṯarti to Alalpi.

First time Albrecht went, some of them, Pintupi mob, never seen white men, they were frightened. For a lot of them, he was the first white man they saw, didn't know why he came, most white people came for trouble.

Jimmy Jugadai

1930: Pastor Albrecht, Martin and Hesekiel made the first trip west.
1931: Second trip west. Titus and Rolf made a base camp at Puṯarti.
1932: Pastor Albrecht visited base at Puṯarti. Took more rations.
1934: Pastor Albrecht again took rations to base at Puṯarti.
1935: Evangelists' camp moved from Puṯarti to Alalpi.
1936: Dr Duguid from Adelaide accompanied Pastor's trip west.
1938: In Melbourne, Albert Namatjira had his first big exhibition.
1939: Pastor Albrecht visited Pitjantjatjara in the Petermann Range.

Titus with some of the people at Alalpi.

Anangu Come to Camp at Alalpi

Through all these years, the Anangu continued to be squeezed out of their country by the cattle stations. As well as finding it increasingly hard to get food, they lived in fear of attack by police and pastoralists. Some Anangu felt it might be safer to live together in larger groups, and under the protection of the Mission. And so people started gradually coming to the evangelists' camp at Alalpi, at the edge of Haasts Bluff.

In 1940, when Pastor Albrecht visited, he counted over a hundred adults living there, and about the same number of children. There were Pintupi people in the west camp, Pitjantjatjara in the south, Warlpiri in the north, and Luritja and Arrente people to the east.

Wati tjilpi kutjungku kulira watjanu,
'Ngalya yarraya, tjukurrpa kulilkitjangku!'
Kamutulutjananya yaltirra ngalya katingu,
Ngurra panya Yilypililanguru.

Yirrititja tjutaya kulira wiyarringu.
Yiwarra kutjupa kutjupa wanaraya wiyarringu.
Ngananalpila wangka ngaatjanya kulintjaku!
Tjiitjulu wangka tjunutja.

Kuwarri Tjiitjunyala kutju wanala!
Yiwarra kutjupanya nyakula wantima!
Tjiitjunya ngananala kutu wanantjaku!
Palurunta katiku ngurraku.
Palurunta katiku ngurraku.

Kamutu brought his family to live at Haasts Bluff.
This hymn tells the story.
It was composed by five of his grandchildren:
Desmond Phillipus, Charlotte Phillipus, Patricia Phillipus,
Mary Malbunka and Gregory Tjupurrula.

One old man heard and said:
'Come and listen to the word of God!'
Kamutu brought us Luritja people
From a place called Ilypili.

The people who heard his message found the way.
Others followed a wrong direction and lost the way.
Every one of us should believe the words
That Jesus has written.

Today we only follow Jesus.
Look and leave the wrong way.
Jesus is the one to follow.
He will take you home.
He will take you home.

Depot at Haasts Bluff

Over the years, other A̲nangu had moved to the township at Alice Springs, where they lived in camps on the Todd River. Pastor Albrecht believed it was better for people to stay in the bush. He kept asking the Government to set aside areas where A̲nangu could live and hunt without interference. In 1941, the land around Haasts Bluff became a reserve.

However, there was not enough bush tucker nearby to feed all the people living there. So Pastor Albrecht made a deal with the Government. If they paid for rations, the Mission would set up a depot at Haasts Bluff, and give out food to supplement the bush food. At first about sixty people got rations there, but the number grew. By 1944, there were about 450 A̲nangu living at Haasts Bluff. There wasn't enough water for so many people.

The ration depot at Haasts Bluff in 1941.

1939: World War II started. Australia at war with Germany and Japan.
1940: A lot of soldiers in Alice Springs. Road to Darwin sealed.
1941: Area around Haasts Bluff became a Reserve.
1941: Ration Depot and Mission Store set up at Haasts Bluff.
1943: Mission built new road from Hermannsburg to Haasts Bluff.
1943: Mission started ration depot for Pitjantjatjara at Areyonga.

A Haasts Bluff family at their home.

In 1943, an Arrente man called Manasse surveyed and built a new road from Hermannsburg to Haasts Bluff. Now the journey only took 5 hours by truck.

Haasts Bluff Settlement

After World War II finished, the Federal Government decided to get more involved with Aboriginal administration. They wanted the ration depot at Haasts Bluff to become a proper settlement. In 1946, they paid for drilling a bore.

At the same time, Pastor Albrecht got some old army huts to use as buildings, and the first church was built. Soon there was a school as well. The Anangu continued to live in their camps, which were oriented towards their traditional country. With hundreds of people living close together, it was easy for diseases to spread. In 1948, many adults and children got very sick with the measles. The next year, a canteen was set up to provide regular meals.

Around 1950, another long period of drought began. Those Anangu who had stayed in their country found it harder and harder to survive. They were also finding it difficult to fulfil the law of the land, because there were not enough other people for ceremonies. Another problem was finding the right marriage partners. So more Anangu came in to Haasts Bluff, to be with family.

Meanwhile rockets were being tested over the desert. The Government did not want Anangu to be living in the missile pathway. They sent patrol officers to clear Anangu out of the test area.

1945: World War II ended.
1946: Government took a greater role in running Haasts Bluff.
1946: Settlement established for Warlpiri at Yuendumu.
1947: Scientists began testing rockets and missiles at Woomera.
1948: Measles epidemic at Haasts Bluff.
1949: Community kitchen was set up at Haasts Bluff.
1950: Federal Government began to support Aboriginal education.
1950s: A bad period of drought. Bush tucker and waterholes depleted.

*When I was a little girl I stayed at Haasts Bluff.
We used to go out on donkeys to pick bush
tomatoes.*

Narli Nakamarra

I was born in the creek

vegetable garden...

School

Canteen

Road to Browns Bore

church

water tank

ration place

road to Alice Springs

Whitefella's house

cg R room

creek

Stockyard

BLUFF

I was 5 year old when I went to Papunya

HAASTS

In this map, Mary Malbunka shows how Haasts Bluff looked when she was young.

People Move to Papunya

In 1951, the Government developed the Assimilation Policy. This meant that Aboriginal people were to be made to live like white people. The Government wanted Anangu to be gathered together in one big settlement, to learn whitefeller ways. Water was short again in Haasts Bluff, so the Government started looking for a better spot. About forty kilometres north of Haasts Bluff they found a place where there was plenty of water under the ground.

This place was close to where the honey ant dreaming tracks meet at Warumpi Hill. It was bordered by Pintupi and Luritja land to the west, Arrente and Pitjantjatjara land to the south, Warlpiri land to the north, and Anmatyerre land to the north and east. It was named Papunya.

In 1956, building began at the new settlement. By 1959, there were well over 700 Anangu living in Papunya. In 1963, the Government began to send trucks out, to make the rest of the Pintupi come in from the desert. Nosepeg Tjupurrula went with the Pintupi Patrols, so that people would be less afraid when they saw their first whitefellers. When the patrols arrived back at the Town Hall, the new settlers were welcomed with ceremonies. Of the seventy-four Pintupi brought in during 1963–64, thirty-five died within a couple of years.

1951: Government developed Assimilation Policy.
1953: Atomic testing began in the desert at Emu, near Milimi.
1956: Government began to establish Papunya settlement.
1956: Atom bombs set off at Maralinga. Continued until 1963.
1957: Evans expedition to Lake Mackay – contact with Pintupi.
1958: Gun Barrel Highway opened up Pintupi lands to welfare patrols.
1959: Official opening ceremony held at Papunya.
1960: Papunya School started and the first church was built.
1963: Some aluminium houses were built for Anangu at Papunya.
1967: Referendum: Australians voted 'Yes' to Aboriginal citizenship; People were given 'sit down money' instead of rations.

The Government buildings and houses for the whitefellers were inside a high fence. The Anangu camped around the fence, facing their traditional country. Many Anangu saw Papunya as a 'mix up place', where people from different *ngurra* and language groups were all mixed up.

Three times a day, people lined up at the kitchen with their pannikins to get their food. Prayers were said, then families ate together at tables.

Pictures were shown once a week. In the recreation room there were two trampolines. The swimming pool was like a tank.

The little farm had sheep and horses as well as vegetables. Some people worked at the farm or in the kitchen, but there was no proper pay. Anangu did not have cars, so they could not go far to hunt or to get bush tucker.

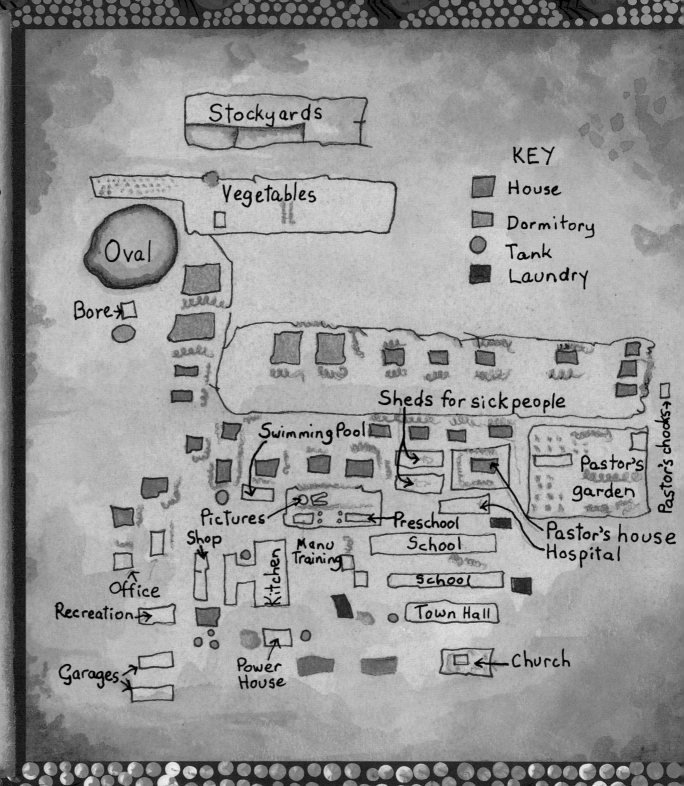

Stockyards

Vegetables

Oval

Bore→

Swimming Pool

Sheds for sick people

Pastor's garden

Pastor's chooks→

Pastor's house

Hospital

Pictures

Preschool

Shop

Manu Training

School

Office

Recreation→

Kitchen

School

Town Hall

Garages→

Power House

Church

KEY
House
Dormitory
Tank
Laundry

Papunya School Starts

In 1960, the school started at Papunya. In those days, children had to have a shower and change into uniforms when they came to school. Then they lined up and went into their classrooms. At the end of the day, children put their camp clothes on again.

At this time, children were not allowed to speak their own language at school. They were meant to learn only the whitefeller way of doing things. Teachers were very strict, and the Tjulkura did not talk to the community about how it wanted the children to learn. The education system did not recognise that A̲nangu elders and families had been teaching children since the *Tjukurrpa*. Teachers did not recognise the learning that the children brought from the community. They did not value learning about country. Children were meant to leave their A̲nangu knowledge with their camp clothes when they arrived.

The pre-school was in an old army hut.

I shifted to Papunya, where I began my schooling. It was there I began to understand the way things were. I realised we were living in a different world now. It was someone else's world.

Smithy Zimran Tjampitjinpa

Going on Bush Trips

In the 1970s, the school occasionally made bush trips to Ulumparru, twenty kilometres south of Papunya, where a dam had been built to hold water from a spring. People grew vegetables and raised pigs and goats out there, to provide food for the settlement. On bush trips the students got food in the traditional way.

There was a big school truck. We used to go in that truck to Ulumparru. We would play in the water there, and some girls would dig for katjutarri close by. We used to eat apuralyi there too. The older ones used to go a long way to get pura. They got ipalu as well. They used to get those foods there, in that bushy country.

When we finished playing in the water, we would eat dinner. The whitefeller teachers would provide meat and food and cool drinks there for us.

Then we would go again and play and swim in the water. We would stay all afternoon in that place. Then we would come back again to Papunya.

Elva Poulson

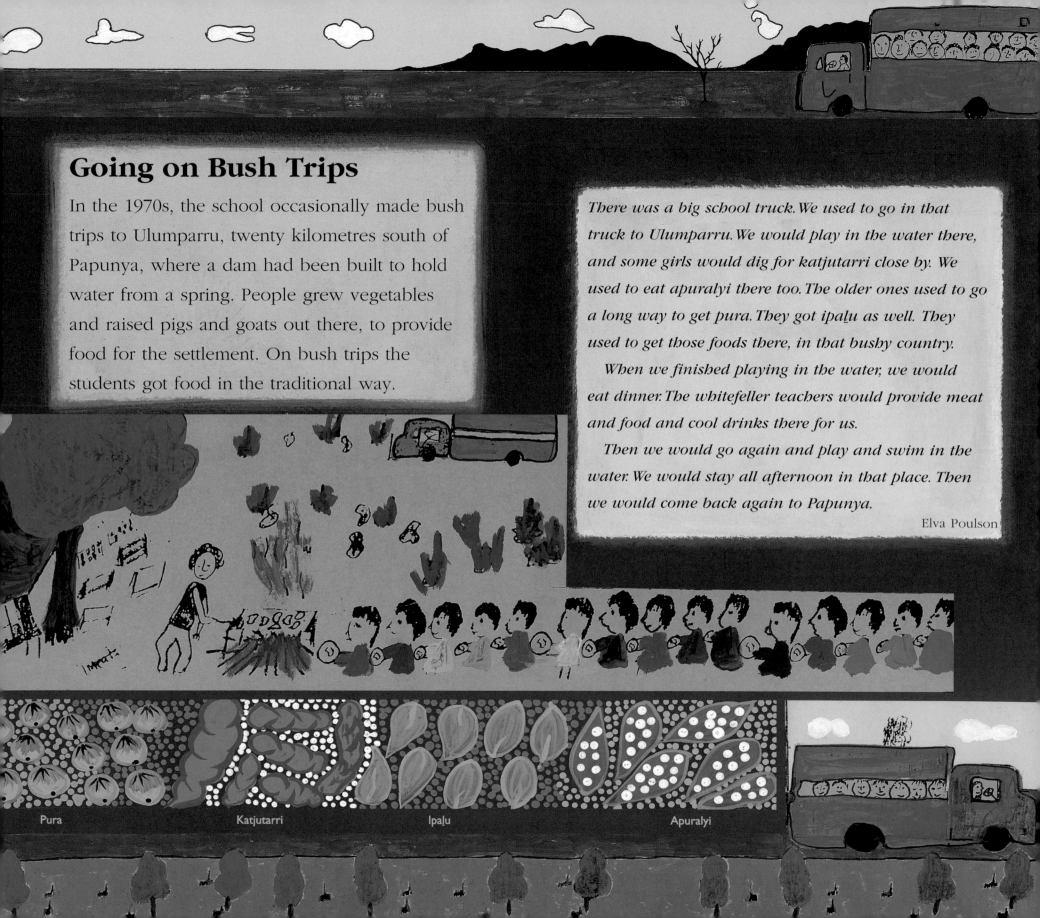

Pura   Katjutarri   Ipalu   Apuralyi

Papunya Art Movement Begins

By 1970, there were about 1400 people living in Papunya. A white Superintendent was in charge of everything. At the school, there were fourteen white teachers, as well as the Anangu assistant teachers. Some men, such as Long Jack Phillipus and Bill Stockman, worked as yardmen at the school.

One of the white teachers, called Geoffrey Bardon, was different from most of the others. He encouraged the children to do art in their traditional way. He also asked them to paint murals to decorate the school walls. When the men saw what was happening in the art classes, they offered to paint the murals. As they came to the big wall at the entrance, Kaapa Tjampitjimpa began to paint honey ants.

'Are these proper Aboriginal honey ants?' Geoffrey Bardon asked. 'Nothing is to be whitefeller.'

'Not ours,' Kaapa replied. 'Yours.'

'Paint yours,' the teacher said. 'Anangu honey ants.'

So Kaapa went and talked to Long Jack and Bill Stockman and the other men. Then they all began to paint the honey ants in the traditional way.

Honey ant mural at Papunya School, 1971.

Mural at Papunya School, 1971.

After the men painted the honey ant mural, they realised that they could use acrylic paint to depict the stories that they used to paint with ochre on their bodies or make in huge sand mosaics. The men immediately began to paint their stories onto canvas or board. Through painting, they remembered their country. These pictures were like title deeds, showing which people belonged to which country.

Over the next few months, more and more men started painting with the new materials. They worked in the Town Hall, and the art teacher took the paintings to Alice Springs and sold them for the men.

When white people down south began to see Papunya paintings, they wanted to buy them. But once the pictures were sold, the stories could be seen by the wrong people.

Another problem was that the Superintendent and some other Government people at Papunya did not want the men to be painting instead of working as labourers. They did not like Anangu to be independent. Some of them thought that the paintings were by 'Government Aborigines' and were therefore 'Government paintings'. Soon the honey ant mural at the school was painted over.

Of course, the Papunya men kept painting, and women also started painting their stories onto canvas. As time went on, the artists made an agreement with each other. Some stories were all right to tell outside the community, but other stories were to be kept secret.

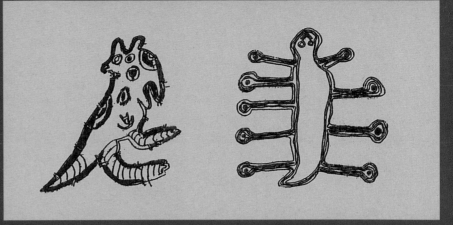
Designs by Amos and Nita, Papunya School, 1971.

A group of artists with Geoffrey Bardon outside the Town Hall, 1971.

1970: American space station opened at Pine Gap, near Alice Springs.
1971: Papunya Art Movement began at Papunya School.
      Painting men formed Papunya Artists' Co-operative.
1972: Papunya Artists' Co-operative got name 'Papunya Tula'.
1972: Aboriginal Embassy, Canberra. Aboriginal flag flown.
1975: Up north, Gurindji won land rights to Wattie Creek.
1976: Northern Territory Land Rights Act.
1979: Obed Raggett became the first Anangu pastor at Papunya.

People Move to Outstations

Within a few years of being settled at Papunya, many Anangu were keen to move away again. Some people wanted to go back and look after their traditional country. Some did not like living in a crowded settlement. Others wanted to get away from Government supervisors. This led to the outstation movement. As early as 1966, a number of Pintupi moved to Alumbra Bore.

Over the years, the Pintupi moved further west, using the outstations like stepping stones back to their country. In 1978, they reached Watiyawanu (Mt Liebig). In 1981, they pushed west through Ilypili to Walungurru (Kintore).

By this time, Papunya School was also running a school at Mt Liebig. There was no building, but about fifty children gathered for lessons under a tree. A health worker visited once a week from Papunya.

The Government did not want a school at Kintore because they did not want to encourage people to move there. At first a couple of Papunya teachers camped at the outstation, and held lessons in the shelter of a corrugated iron windbreak. By 1985, Kintore had its own health service. The school had two tin sheds and four teachers.

1975: 300 people lived in five outstations near Papunya.
1977: 500 people lived in eight outstations near Papunya.
1979: Sixteen outstations were occupied near Papunya.
The picture on p. 35 shows the outstations around Papunya.

Kids collected tin cans to raise money for Kintore School, 1986.

Mt Liebig Clinic, 1982.

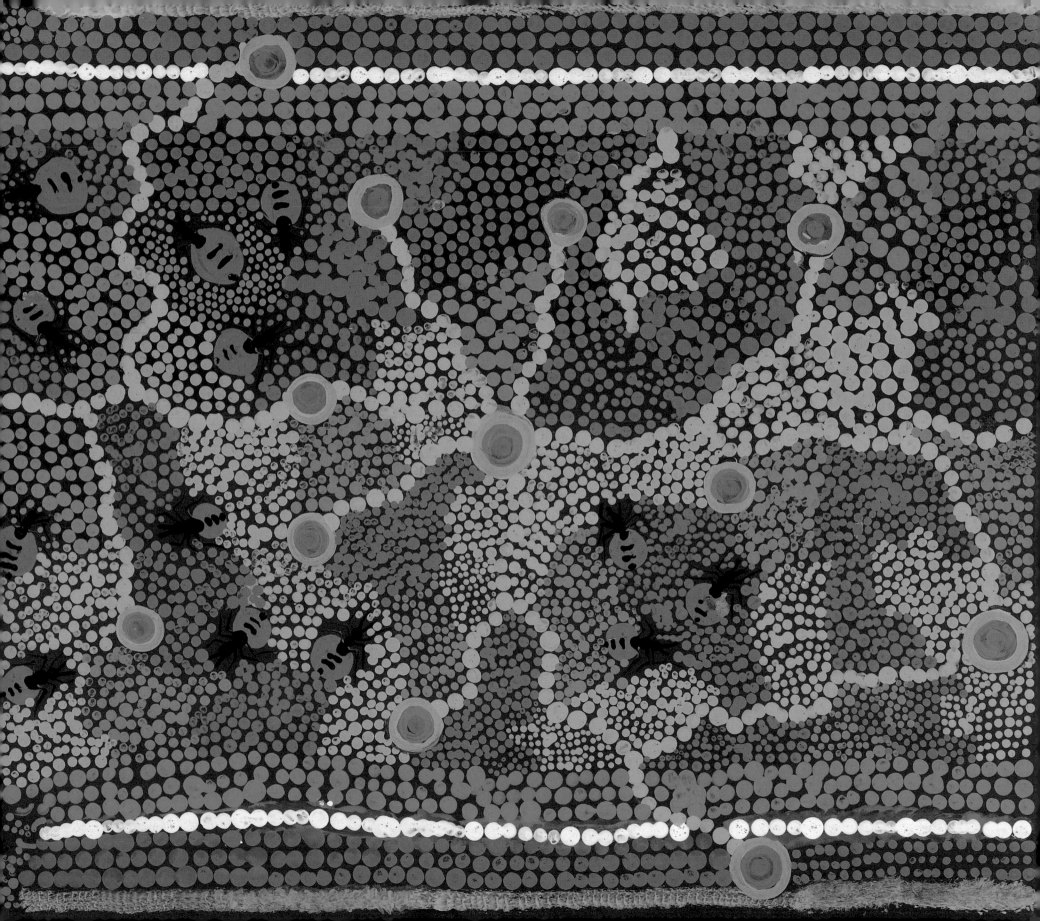

Papunya Famous for Music

Since the *Tjukurrpa*, Anangu have been recording their history in songs and music. During the twentieth century, they started playing contemporary music as well.

In 1981, the Warumpi Band got together at Papunya. Soon the group began to tour Aboriginal communities in the Northern Territory and Western Australia. In 1983, the band recorded their first single. The songs were 'Jailanguru Pakarnu' ('Out from Jail') and 'Kintorelakutu' ('Going to Kintore'). This was the first rock single sung in an Aboriginal language. In 1984 Warumpi Band put out their first album – *Big Name, No Blankets*. The band's original songs gave messages about the danger of alcohol, as well as celebrating the land.

By the mid 1980s, the Warumpi Band was recognised as one of Australia's leading rock bands. They played in Sydney and up the east coast. In 1986 the band joined with Midnight Oil for the *Blackfella-Whitefella* tour of northern and inland Australia.

The Warumpi Band has made Papunya famous for music, just as the painting movement made Papunya famous for art.

Yuwa! Ngurra palya!
Nganampa ngurra watjalpayi kuya
Nganampa ngurra watjalpayi kuya
Nganampa ngurra tjanampa wiya!
Nganampa ngurra Warumpinya!
Yuwa! Ngurra palya!

'Warumpinya' ('Papunya')
from *Big Name, No Blankets*
Sammy Butcher, Neil Murray

Yes! Good home!
They always say our place is bad
They always say our home is no good
It's our place, not theirs!
It's our home, Papunya!
Yes! Good home!

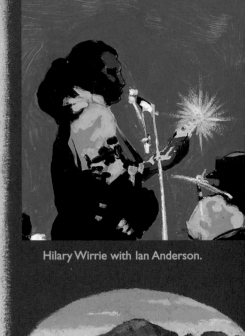

Hilary Wirrie with Ian Anderson.

Left to right: Sid (roadie), Neil Murray (guitarist), Gordon Butcher (drums), George Rurrambu (singer), Sammy Butcher (lead guitar), David Cook (Manager).

Papunya Famous for Art

During the 1980s, art galleries all over the world began to buy and exhibit Papunya paintings. Through seeing Anangu stories told on canvas, some whitefellers started to understand a little bit about why land is so important to Aboriginal people.

In 1988, Michael Nelson was asked to design a mosaic for the area in front of the new Parliament House in Canberra. Papunya dancing women danced *Inma* at the Opening Ceremony. Now whenever politicians go to Parliament to makes laws, they are reminded of Aboriginal culture.

Yes, in the old days people never show their paintings. But now there is a new way of life ... Now we want to show our paintings to everybody; show them to the world. We want to tell people that this is an important place to us. This is land! They have taken it away from us and they didn't even think about it! This is the reason why we want to show the world our Dreamtime culture, so that they can understand our way of life. They are probably starting to think back now on what has been happening to Aboriginal people.

Michael Jagamara Nelson

37

Building up Papunya

Over the 1980s, Papunya developed, as Anangu took more control over their own community.

In 1980, a big community meeting voted that Papunya should be dry. All the bottles of alcohol were taken to the rifle range and shot.

Through this decade the Papunya Housing Association did a lot of work building houses for people. A new church was built and three new Anangu pastors were ordained. Papunya also became strong in football and softball.

PAPUNYA. N.T.

Tjakulpa

MONDAY...SEVENTEENTH...NOVEMBER...1980   PRICE...20 CENTS

PAPUNYA NOW DRY.

Boys learning Puulapa.

Girls learning Inma.

At Papunya School at this time, a number of books were made in Pintupi and Luritja, collecting stories from community members. Aboriginal Culture was taught on Wednesday afternoons. Girls learned *Inma*, and boys learned *Puulapa*.

Power to Papunya!

In the 1990s, Papunya hit the newspaper headlines again, as the community took action to control their own lives. The first battle became known as the Power Dispute.

When the Government had first set up Papunya, electricity was free. In 1992, the Government suddenly said that Anangu would have to pay electricity bills every three months. Papunya people asked to pay by putting tokens into a meter box as they used the power. The Government said no.

One morning in May, electricity workers came very early and cut off Papunya's generator, without consultation. All through that winter, Papunya had no electricity for heat or light. The community held strong, although it had no outside support. In the end, Papunya agreed to sign up for power, but the Government agreed to the tokens. Now all communities pay for power with tokens.

People gather for the dedication of the new church, 1982.

Old style ngurra.

New style ngurra.

1976: Alison Anderson became Community Advisor.
1978: Papunya Council formed.
1979: First issue of Papunya newspaper, *Tjakulpa*, printed.
1981: Warumpi Band formed.
1988: Papunya men went to New York to make a sand mosaic.
1988: In Sydney, Aboriginal protestors rallied against Bicentenary.
1992: Papunya Power Dispute.

A New Vision for Papunya School

By 1992, the community was not happy with the teaching at the school, so parents kept their children at home. The school had to close. In August 1992, community members wrote down their requirements for a partnership between community, council and school. After this, the school got a new principal, called Diane de Vere, who valued Indigenous learning and the role of the Anangu teachers. A new way of working began. In 1994, the School Vision Painting showed everyone the way forward.

This is our painting telling the story of how we want our school to run and how we want our children to learn. It is a story inspired by a painting from Walungurru that we presented at a national curriculum conference.

Our painting tells Anangu teachers' vision for education at Papunya. The centre of our painting shows our original country. The Anangu long ago, before the Tjulkura came, are living in their land. The children learn about their dreamings, their language, their ceremonies, their country – all this is passed on to them by their grandmothers and grandfathers. The diagonal tracks link the culture and language that is taught both at home and in the bush. The tracks shows that people came from a long way away to Papunya with their knowledge and their laws. The honey ants show that Papunya is situated where the honey ant dreaming tracks meet at Warumpi Hill. This is the Tjukurrpa for Papunya and everyone here shares this dreaming. It brings the people together.

The top left-hand corner shows Anangu learning Tjulkura language, and at the same time some of the children and adults learn about grog and petrol sniffing, and some of the elders are worried that Anangu have learned too much Tjulkura culture and have forgotten their own culture. At this time the school ways and decisions were made by Tjulkura, they made the decisions for how and what the children learned. The Anangu culture was kept out of the school. Anangu were not involved. All the decisions were made outside the community without asking Anangu what they wanted for their children.

The bottom right-hand corner shows how we are going to control our own school with Anangu people in charge of our children so that they will be able to come to school and learn properly, and learn both ways education.

At Papunya we now know about schools and now we will make decisions about how and what we want the children to learn. Tjulkura will sit outside and behind Anangu to assist and work with Anangu teachers, students and administrators. If the Tjulkura remain solely in charge, our children will not learn properly at all.

At present the Anangu and Tjulkura teachers are working out together how to operate the school.

Murphy Tjupurulla Roberts, Charlotte Napurulla Phillipus, Linda Nakamarra Anderson, Sabrina Nakamarra Kantawarra, Dennis Tjakamarra Nelson, Narlie Nakamarra Nelson, Mary-Anne Nakamarra Nelson.

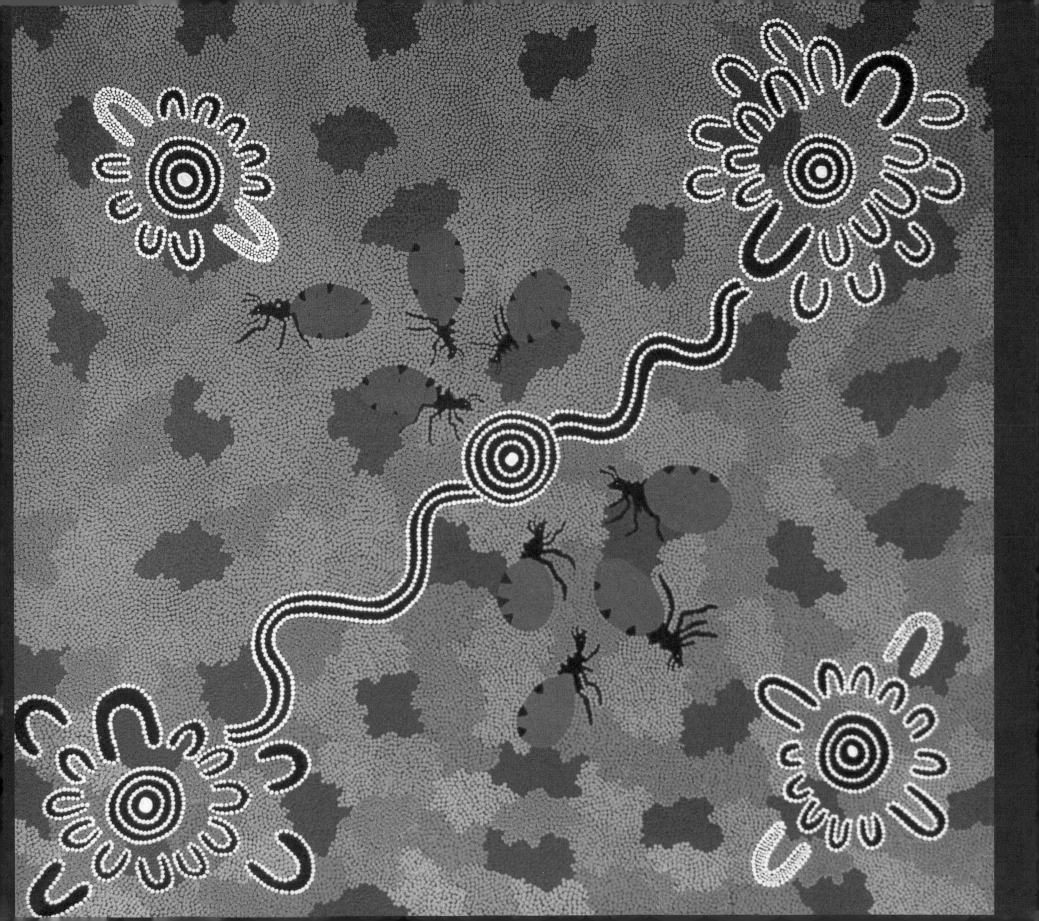

Winning Back Country

Since the Tjulkura first came to Australia, Aboriginal people have fought to get their land back. One of the main difficulties was to get white people to understand the way in which country belonged to different groups of people, and the way in which people belonged to their country.

During the 1990s, Aboriginal people for the first time had their rights to country recognised in whitefeller law. In 1992, a man named Eddie Mabo, from Murray Island in the Torres Strait, went to the High Court in Canberra to claim his right to his traditional country. In the Mabo Decision, the judges agreed that Australia was not *terra nullius* – no one's land – when the Tjulkura arrived. Two years later, this was confirmed when the Wik people went to court.

These legal decisions helped A̲nangu win back a tiny bit of their country.

Women dance Inma at the ceremony when Karrinyarra is handed back.

Seventy kilometres north of Papunya there is the sacred site of Pulka Karrinyarra, at the mountain that Tjulkura call Central Mt Wedge. When the traditional owners tried to establish an outstation on the property in the early 1990s, they faced strong opposition from the Northern Territory Cattlemen's Association.

In 1995, the lease for Central Mt Wedge was purchased on behalf of Luritja, Anmateyerre and Warlpiri traditional owners. A land claim under the Land Rights Act was then lodged. In 1996, during a court hearing that lasted a week, two hundred claimants showed the Aboriginal Land Commissioner the many sites in this area. They performed songs and ceremonies to show that this had been their country since the *Tjukurrpa*. Over the next three years, as the legal business went on, traditional owners sat down at Mt Wedge. In July 1999, the Governor-General, Sir William Deane, handed back the former pastoral lease to traditional owners under the Aboriginal Land Rights Act.

This painting is women's dreaming for Karrinyarra. It shows the nulla nulla in the centre with all sorts of mangarri around it. The semicircles are women sitting down digging for food. As they dig they sing the songs for Karrinyarra.

There is water there at Karrinyarra — running water from the rocks, and a big lake. And you can dig down for water for drinking. Lots of mangarri grows there, so a lot of people have always gone there for ceremonies.

For a long time we didn't have Karrinyarra, and now we have got it back. The traditional owners are happy to get Karrinyarra back. It is important to show the children and teach them about country there.

Emma Nungarrayi
Traditional owner, Karrinyarra

Papunya School Tells its Story

In the last years of the twentieth century, Papunya School became stronger and stronger, as Anangu and Tjulkura teachers followed the way of learning set out in the Vision Painting. At Papunya School now we have our own curriculum. At the centre we have country, of course! A special part of the curriculum is learning about the history of our country.

Each year our school makes a couple of country visits, to different *ngurra*. Community members come with us, and we camp for two or three nights. When we are out there, our elders tell us the *yara* – stories – for that particular country. They teach us the right songs and dances, and they paint us up in the right way for those dances. They show us where the waterholes are, and how to dig for water. They teach us how to find things to eat.

These jigsaws show how we learn through both knowledge systems when we study Animals, Plants and Seasons.

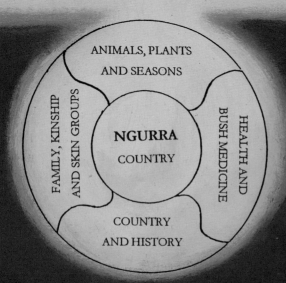

ANIMALS, PLANTS AND SEASONS

FAMILY, KINSHIP AND SKIN GROUPS

NGURRA

COUNTRY

HEALTH AND BUSH MEDICINE

COUNTRY AND HISTORY

1992: School Boycott: Enrolments dropped to 18.
Community set out Minimum Requirements of Education.

1992: High Court: Mabo Decision revoked *terra nullius*.

1994: Papunya School Vision Painting.

1995: Papunya School set up site-based Teacher Education in association with Batchelor College.

1997: *Bringing Them Home:* Report on Stolen Children.

1998: Linda Allen completed Diploma of Education.

1999: Charlotte Phillipus, Monica Robinson completed Dip Ed.

1999: Traditional owners won Land Rights to Central Mt Wedge.

2000: Hundreds of thousands of Australians marched for Reconciliation.

2001: *Papunya School Book of Country and History* published!

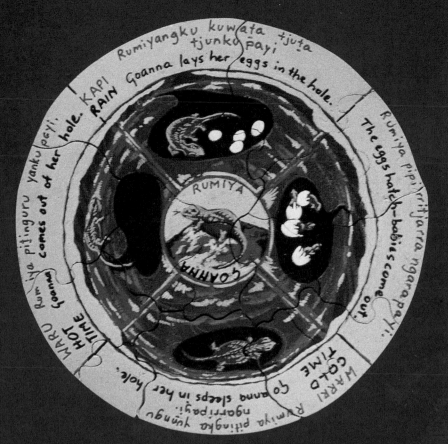

At school we learn two ways – A̲nangu way and Western way. But most of what we need to know isn't written down on paper. That's why we have to make our own books, telling our own stories of country and history.

Maybe Papunya might become famous for making books, just like it is famous for music and art!

The book above folds out to show some of the things in our community. The book below teaches us to track goanna.

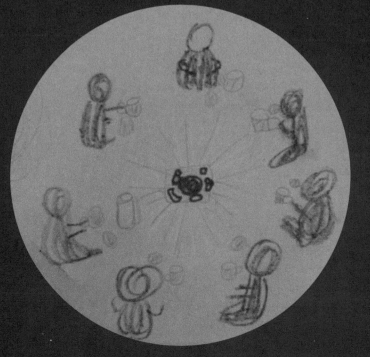

We want to see the children, after being educated at Papunya School, coming out like honey ants full of honey - nice and healthy honey - not poison inside. We want to see the children learning both ways, and coming out bright orange and yellow together, like honey ants.

Linda Kapunani Allen

45

Since the time of the *Tjukurrpa*, Anangu have been living in their country and looking after it.

Anangu obey the law of the land.

Arrente live in their traditional country.

Anmatyerre live in their traditional country.

The balance of nature is intact.

Anangu look after the country.

Pitjantjatjara live in their traditional country.

Pintupi live in their traditional country.

1947 Woomera rocket testing.

1950

1941 Anangu start to be given rations at Haasts Bluff.

1946 Government drills bore at Haasts Bluff.

1951 Assimilation Policy.

Drought years. Anangu find less and less bush tucker.

1967 Referendum on Aboriginal Citizenship.

Anangu elders teach children the paintings about country.

Anangu elders teach children the stories about country.

Water bad at Haasts Bluff. Government drills a bore 40km north, near Warumpi. Wants all the Anangu to move there.

1960

Anangu elders teach children the dances about country.

Anangu elders teach children the songs about country.

By 1959, 700 Anangu are sitting down at Papunya.

1960 Papunya School starts.

Pintupi patrols bring people in to Papunya.